A New True Book

URANUS

By Dennis B. Fradin

CP CHILDRENS PRESS®
CHICAGO

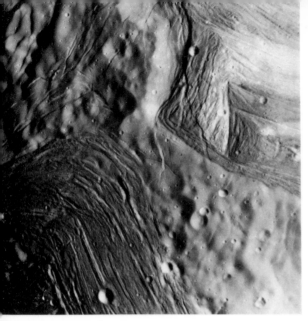

Voyager 2 photographed the surface of Miranda, a moon orbiting Uranus.

PHOTO CREDITS
AP/Wide World Photos—37
Art—John Forsberg—8-9
The Bettmann Archive—21, 22, 29
Finley Holiday Film Corporation—13
Historical Pictures Service, Chicago—19
Art—Len Meents—32
NASA—2, 6, 12 (center), 31
NASA-JET PROPULSION LAB—Cover, 11 (2 photos), 12 (top), 39, 41, 42, 43
National Optical Astronomy Observatories—18
North Wind Picture Archives—15
Chart courtesy Odyssey Magazine—10
Photri—4, 12 (bottom), 17, 24, 26, 33 (2 photos), 34 (2 photos), 45
Cover—Painting shows *Voyager 2* passing Uranus on its journey toward Neptune.

Library of Congress Cataloging-in-Publication Data

Fradin, Dennis B.
  Uranus / by Dennis B. Fradin

    p.   cm. — (A new true book)
  Includes index.
  Summary: Discusses the seventh planet, how it was named, and the information astronomers have gathered about it.
    ISBN 0-516-01177-4
    1. Uranus (Planet)—Juvenile
literature. [1. Uranus (Planet)] I. Title.
QB681.F73   1989   89-9984
523.4'7—dc20   CIP
                      AC

TABLE OF CONTENTS

STARS

There are millions of stars in space. We can see several thousand stars at night with just our eyes. Telescopes reveal millions more.

All the stars but one can be seen only at night. The one daytime star is the Sun. Light from the Sun gives us our daytime.

The Sun and all the other stars are giant balls

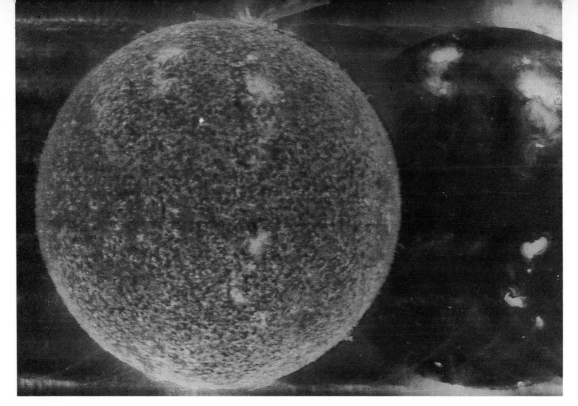

The Sun is a star.

of hot, glowing gas. They
shine by their own light.
The Sun is just an
average star in size. It
looks so big because it
is so much closer to us
than the other stars.

PLANETS

   Planets are large objects
that orbit (move around)
stars. Many stars besides
the Sun may have planets.
But we know the most about
the Sun's family of nine
planets.

   Hot Mercury is the nearest
planet to the Sun. Then come
Venus, Earth, Mars, Jupiter,
and Saturn. Uranus comes
seventh. Neptune is eighth,
and frozen Pluto is ninth.

There are three ways to spot planets. First, planets don't twinkle, or flicker. Stars seem to twinkle because Earth's air interferes with the small point of light that comes from a faraway star. But the planets are closer to Earth, so the disk of light

from them is larger. Planets
don't twinkle because the
Earth's air has less effect
on the way we see a
larger disk of light.

Second, planets seem to
move among the stars
over time. This happens
because the planets are
orbiting the Sun.

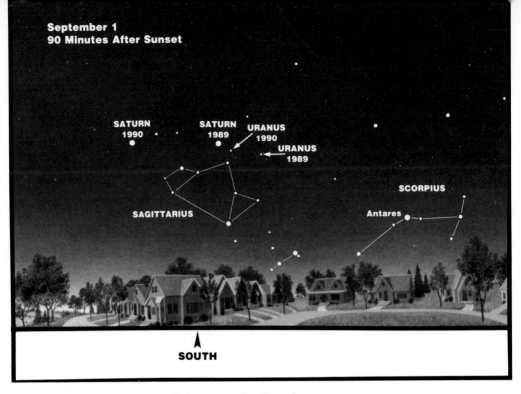

SATURN 1990

SATURN 1989

URANUS 1990

URANUS 1989

SCORPIUS

SAGITTARIUS

Antares

SOUTH

Astronomers make maps of the stars in the sky.

There is a third way to find the planets. You can get a special sky map. Astronomy magazines have them. These maps show where to spot the planets at any given time.

10

THE FIVE PLANETS OF THE ANCIENTS

Ancient people thought there were just five planets— Mercury, Venus, Mars, Jupiter, and Saturn. All five are bright enough to be seen with just our eyes.

On about thirty-five days a year, Mercury can be seen near sunset or sunrise. The

Mariner 10 photographs of Mercury (left) and Venus (right)

Mars

Saturn

Jupiter

white planet Venus is the brightest object in the sky besides the Sun and the Moon. Mars is nicknamed the "red planet" because of its color. If you see a red heavenly body that does not twinkle, it is Mars.

Jupiter is bright and yellow-white. Saturn is not

quite as bright as Jupiter and is a bit more yellowish.

The ancients did not spot Uranus. And they never saw Neptune and Pluto. It takes a telescope to see those three planets.

What about our home planet, Earth? Anyone can

Earth

Copernicus showed that the Sun is just one among many millions of stars. He proved that the planets orbit the Sun. The Sun and its planets are the main members of what became known as the Solar System. The Solar System can be thought of as the Sun's "family" of objects.

Moons are part of the Solar System, too. Moons are objects that orbit most

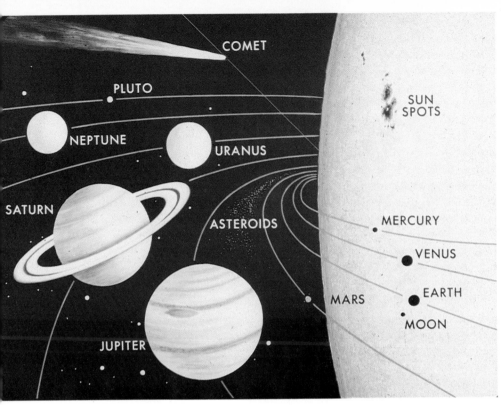

COMET

PLUTO

NEPTUNE

URANUS

SUN SPOTS

SATURN

ASTEROIDS

MERCURY

VENUS

MARS

EARTH

MOON

JUPITER

Our Solar System is made up of planets, moons, asteroids, and comets.

of the planets. Comets are also part of the Solar System. They travel in long orbits around the Sun. Comets are made of ice, gas, and dust. They have long, glowing tails when they are near the Sun.

This comet, IRAS-Araki-Alcock, was photographed on May 8, 1983. The head of the comet is at the lower left.

Sometimes comets can be seen from Earth.

Copernicus lived before people had telescopes. So he thought there were just six planets—Mercury, Venus, Earth, Mars, Jupiter, and Saturn.

URANUS IS DISCOVERED

Galileo (1564-1642)
with his telescope

The telescope was invented in about 1608. Galileo of Italy was the first famous astronomer to use a telescope. Galileo made many discoveries. He learned that the Milky Way is made of millions of

19

stars. He learned that Jupiter has moons. But he did not find Uranus. Uranus wasn't discovered until William Herschel spotted the planet in 1781.

William Herschel was born in Hannover, Germany. He moved to England around the age of twenty. He earned his living by playing the organ and teaching music. But at about the age of thirty-five, he took up astronomy as a

William Herschel, the discoverer of Uranus, lived from 1738 to 1822. He studied the stars with his sister, Caroline.

hobby. He built telescopes and made great discoveries with them. His sister, Caroline Herschel, worked with him and made some discoveries of her own.

21

Herschel's
forty-foot-long
reflecting
telescope

On the night of March 13, 1781, Herschel was looking for double stars near the border of the constellations Taurus the Bull and Gemini the Twins. He saw an unknown greenish object in this region.

Herschel knew it wasn't
a star. It didn't twinkle.
Also, stars are so distant
from Earth that they look
like points of light even in
a telescope. This object
looked like a little ball.
That is how planets look.

Herschel thought comets
would also look like little
balls when far from the
Sun. So, at first, Herschel
thought he had found a
comet. He wrote papers and
letters about it. This helped
other astronomers find the

Voyager 2
photograph of
Uranus, taken
from 1.7 million
miles away
from the planet

object. Herschel studied
his object many more
times during the next
months. Finally, all the
astronomers agreed.
William Herschel had
discovered planet number
seven! It was the first

discovery of a planet since ancient people had first seen Mercury, Venus, Mars, Jupiter, and Saturn.

Astronomers studied old records. They found that the seventh planet had been seen in telescopes more than twenty times before William Herschel's discovery! The first such sighting had been made back in 1690 by John Flamsteed of England. But Flamsteed and the others

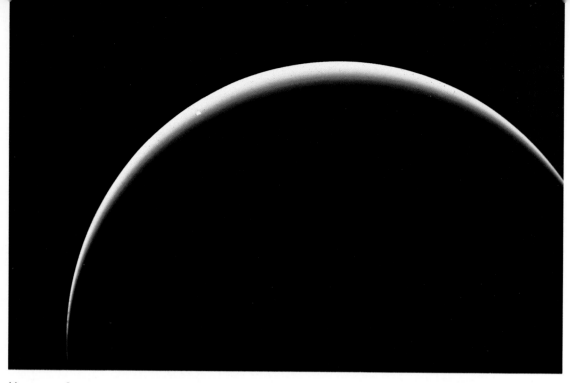

Voyager 2 was 600,000 miles away when it took this photograph of Uranus.

who had seen the seventh planet hadn't known what it was. Herschel was the first to show that it was a planet. That is why we say that Herschel and not Flamsteed discovered Uranus.

NAMING
THE NEW PLANET

At first many people called the new object "Herschel's Planet" or "Herschel." Some people hoped that one of these names would become its official name. One of the many other suggested names was "Dumbbell." Why this strange name? The planet had made dumbbells of astronomers by going undiscovered for so long!

Herschel himself wanted to call it "Georgium Sidus" (George's Star) to honor England's King George III. But many people opposed this name. First, the object was a planet, not a star. Second, many people disliked King George III. When Herschel made his discovery, the American colonies were fighting to break free of George III and English rule.

The other planets had been named for ancient

Like many of the other objects in our Solar System, Uranus was named after an ancient god.

gods and goddesses. Many people thought that the new planet should be, too. Johann E. Bode of Germany liked the name Uranus. It was the name of the ancient Greek god of the sky. Uranus won out as the name of the new planet.

URANUS POINTS THE WAY TO NEPTUNE AND PLUTO

Gravity is the force that holds objects together in space. The Sun's gravity keeps Earth from flying off into space. Earth's gravity keeps the Moon from flying off, and holds us to the ground.

Astronomers soon saw something strange about Uranus. Sometimes it wobbled away from the

Sun. The gravity of something to the outside seemed to be pulling at Uranus. Astronomers thought this something might be an eighth planet. They searched the sky. In 1846 the eighth planet was discovered. It was named Neptune.

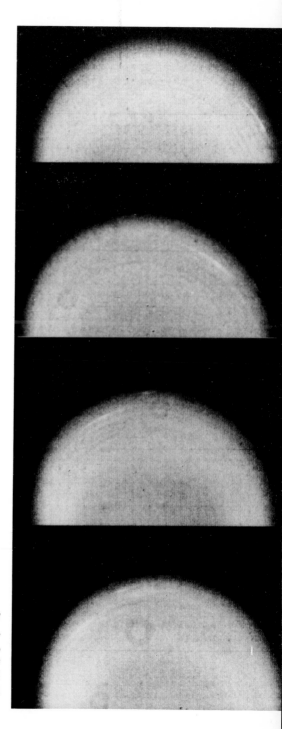

Time-lapse photographs show changing features on Uranus. Do you see the two small, bright, streaky clouds on the top photograph? Can you see how they have moved on the bottom photograph?

Something seemed to be tugging at Neptune from the outside, too. Also, something in addition to Neptune still seemed to be tugging at Uranus. Astronomers searched for a ninth planet. It was found in 1930 and named Pluto.

MERCURY

VENUS

EARTH

MARS

JUPITER

SATURN

URANUS

NEPTUNE

PLUTO

 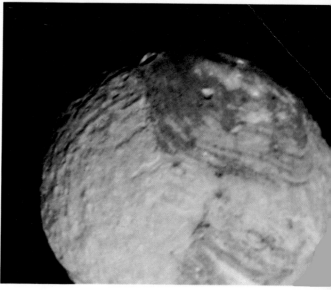

Oberon (left) and Miranda (right) are moons of Uranus.

WHAT TELESCOPES
REVEALED

Telescopes helped
astronomers learn a lot
about Uranus in the 200
years after its discovery. In
1787 William Herschel
discovered two moons of

33

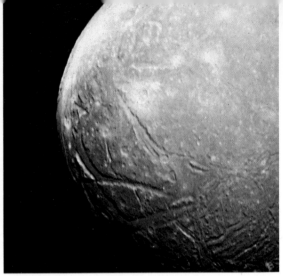

Voyager photographed Titania (left) and Ariel (right), moons of Uranus

Uranus. Two more were found in 1851. Uranus's fifth moon was found in 1948.

Telescopes also showed that Uranus is very big. Of the nine planets, only Jupiter and Saturn are bigger than Uranus. Our Earth could fit inside Uranus over 60 times!

Astronomers found that when we view Uranus, we are not seeing its surface. We are seeing clouds over the planet. These clouds are made of gases that would be poisonous to us. Belts can be seen on the clouds. They do not stretch across the planet from side to side like Jupiter's belts. They go up and down. This is because Uranus is lying on its side as it rotates, or spins.

Astronomers learned that,

in places, the temperature
in Uranus's clouds is
colder than -300° F.
Uranus's atmosphere is so
cold because the planet is
so far from the Sun.
Uranus takes eighty-four
years to orbit the Sun
because of its great
distance. This means that
Uranus's year is eighty-four
earth-years long.

In 1977 astronomers
learned something new
about Uranus. Saturn had
been thought to be the

Uranus was discovered to have rings around it just like Saturn.

only planet with rings.
Uranus was found to have
rings, too. Jupiter was also
found to have a ring about
that time.

37

WHAT *VOYAGER 2* REVEALED

No telescope on Earth can provide a clear picture of Uranus. The planet is too far away. During the mid-1900s, scientists found a way to see the planets up close. They began launching space probes toward the planets. Space probes carry no people. They carry instruments that send photos and data back to Earth.

Painting shows *Voyager 2* passing by Uranus on its journey toward Neptune.

In 1977 the United States launched the *Voyager 1* and *Voyager 2* space probes. The Voyager mission was to study Jupiter, Saturn,

Uranus, and Neptune.

The Voyager probes provided a great deal of new data about Jupiter in 1979. They revealed much about Saturn in 1980-1981. *Voyager 2* then went on to Uranus, and passed near the planet in early 1986. The probe provided a wealth of data about Uranus and its moons.

Astronomers had not known how long Uranus takes to spin one time.

A view of Uranus and its rings as seen from Miranda

Voyager 2 learned that Uranus spins once in about 17¼ hours. This means that a day on Uranus is about 17¼ hours long.

41

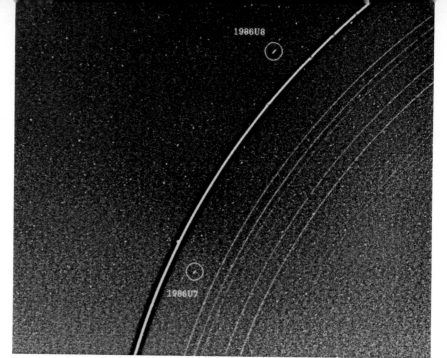

Uranus has nine rings. This photograph shows two of its moons, 1986U8 and 1986U7.

Voyager 2 found ten new little moons of Uranus. This brought Uranus's total to fifteen. Only Saturn and Jupiter have more moons.

Voyager 2 also obtained great views of Uranus's five biggest moons.

Voyager photograph of the rings of Uranus. The stars in the background are streaked because the camera was moved to view the rings.

Uranus's rings were found to be made of large chunks of rock and ice. And it was found that Uranus's atmosphere extends to a depth of about 5,000 miles.

MORE QUESTIONS ABOUT URANUS

Scientists know a lot about Uranus. But they still have many questions. Why is the seventh planet tipped over on its side? Did something slam into Uranus and knock the planet over?

Is Uranus covered by a water ocean over a core of melted rocky material? What formed

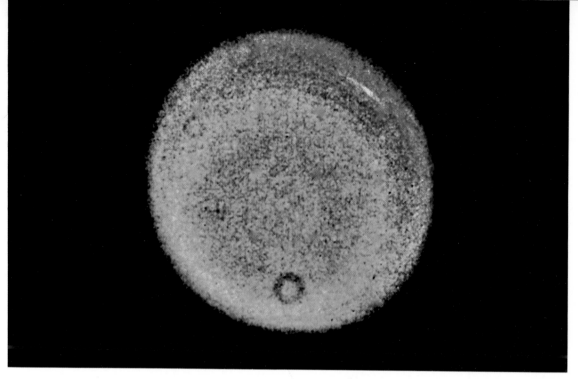
In many ways Uranus is still a mystery.

the rings? Could there be
any life on Uranus?

Someday more probes
will be sent to Uranus. They
will help us learn more
about the distant planet that
William Herschel discovered
more than 200 years ago.

FACTS ABOUT URANUS

Average Distance from Sun— About 1,780,000,000 (one billion, 780 million) miles

Closest Approach to Earth— About 1,700,000,000 (one billion, 700 million) miles

*Diameter—*About 32,000 miles

*Length of Day—*About 17¼ hours

*Length of Year—*About 84 earth-years

*Temperatures—*Places in Uranus's clouds are colder than -300° F; but below the clouds Uranus may have a very hot ocean

*Atmosphere—*Mainly hydrogen, helium, methane

*Number of Moons—*At least 15

*Weight of an Object on Uranus That Would Weigh 100 Pounds on Earth—*93 pounds

*Average Speed as Uranus Orbits the Sun—*About 4 miles per second

WORDS YOU SHOULD KNOW

ancient(AIN • shent)—very old

astronomer(ast • RAH • nih • mer)—a person who studies stars, planets, and other heavenly bodies

atmosphere(AT • muss • feer)—the gases surrounding some heavenly bodies

billion(BILL • yun)—a thousand million (1,000,000,000)

comet(CAHM • it)—an object (made of ice, gas, and dust) that has a long, glowing tail when near the Sun

constellation(kahn • stel • LAY • shun)—a star group in a certain area of the sky

double star(DUB • il STAHR)—two stars that are very close together or that only look like they are very close together

Earth(ERTH)—the planet (the third from the Sun) on which we live

gravity(GRAV • ih • tee)—the force that holds things down to a heavenly body

heavenly body(HEV • en • lee BAHD • ee) — an object in space, such as a star, planet, or moon

hobby(HAH • bee) — something a person does for fun

million(mil • yun) — a thousand thousand (1,000,000)

moon(MOON) — a natural object that orbits a planet; Uranus has at least 15 moons

orbit(OR • bit) — the path an object takes when it moves around another object

planet(PLAN • it) — a large object that orbits a star; the Sun has nine planets

reflect(ree • FLEKT) — to throw back

Solar System(SOH • ler SISS • tim) — the Sun and its "family" of objects

space probe(SPAISS PROHB) — an unmanned spacecraft sent to study heavenly bodies

star(STAHR) — a giant ball of hot, glowing gases

Sun(SUHN) — the yellow star that is the closest star to Earth

telescope(TEL • ih • skohp) — an instrument that makes distant objects look closer

Uranus(YOO • rih • nuss) — the seventh planet from the Sun

Voyager 2(VOY • ih • jer TOO) — a space probe that studied Uranus

INDEX

About the Author

Dennis B. Fradin attended Northwestern University on a partial creative scholarship and was graduated in 1967. His previous books include the Young People's Stories of Our States series for Childrens Press, and Bad Luck Tony *for Prentice-Hall. In the True Book series Dennis has written about astronomy, farming, comets, archaeology, movies, space colonies, the space lab, explorers, and pioneers. He is married and the father of three children.*